ORANGE CHIPMUNKS ROCK

To: Mcleland & Audrey

Faith

by Faith Balsama

Life is almost perfect at Chipmunk Run. Find out what Sako and Suki are up to when they encounter Purple Fuji Mama. Smart and cute as a button, these chipmunks rock.

Their story is told in Zappai which is a form of Japanese poetry rooted in Haiku. Each poem consists of seventeen syllables in three lines of five, seven, and five.

The verses are not technical (like Haiku) and are created for pure reader pleasure and amusement. Enjoy!

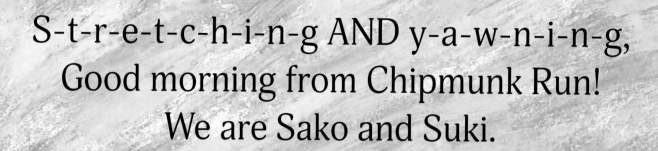

S-t-r-e-t-c-h-i-n-g AND y-a-w-n-i-n-g,
Good morning from Chipmunk Run!
We are Sako and Suki.

Our day has begun.
We celebrate Mister Sun.
He ripens our food.

Oh— did we say food?
Food is ALWAYS on our minds,
We dart here and there.

Rolling and tumbling
Up and down moss-covered rocks,
Seeking and searching.

Scampering around,
Stuffing our fuzzy cheeks full.
WHAT IS that sharp smell?

Beware of the cat
Big Purple Fuji Mama—
She's out for a meal!

We sound the alarm:
CHIP-CHIP, CHIP, CHIP, CHIP-CHIP, CHIP!
Birds fly to the trees.

YIKES!!! HOLY FUR BALLS!
She pounces with claws showing.
We run for our lives.

Deep inside our den
We calm down and rest a while
Hugging each other

Underground we're safe.
Only the earthworms are here
Turning the rich soil.

Our courage restored;
We head out with a whisper,
"Predator alert."

The cat is napping.
Her long whiskers are twitching;
Her paws are moving.

She must be dreaming
Of the prey that got away.
Whew, we are lucky!

Not making a sound,
We follow through with our plan.
Catnip is the goal.

We streak to the patch
Passing by the lily pond—
No time for a drink.

We're running so fast;
Turtles are splashing off logs.
Bullfrogs are jumping.

No time for playing;
The butterflies are tempting
Fluttering around.

Oh no! It's a snake!
Stretched across the trail sunning;
We have to detour.

Buzzing dragonflies
Guide us to the sweet meadow
Where the catnip grows.

We eye up some stalks;
Quickly chew off tender shoots.
To the cat we go.

Still in sweet dreamland,
We tippy toe around her
Dropping stinky leaves.

...PEE-U

As we dash away,
She wakes with her nose crinkling,
What IS this fragrance?

She begins to roll—
Rubbing and eating the herb,
Feeling quite giddy.

Mewing and purring
Drooling all over the place
Totally clueless.

What a crazy cat
Purple Fuji Mama is
A sight to behold.

From a safe distance
We are laughing at our prank.
She will never know.

How clever we are!
Until our next escapade,
Stay alert, Mama.

Thank you for reading
"Orange Chipmunks Rock." To find out
more about the author/illustrator,
please go to www.faithbalsama.com.